Eternal Wings

Qasim Khan

BookLeaf Publishing

India | USA | UK

Dedication

This book, Eternal Wings, is dedicated to two people who gave me the gift of life, love, and unyielding support —my beloved parents.

To my mother, who have always taught me to be determined and courageous in my life. She herself is an epitome of strength and resilience and has instilled in me the same values - never to give up and to try and give my best efforts even if the chances are negligible. To my father, who have taught me to have great ambitions in life and inculcating in me the eternal value that big goals require big sacrifices. To both of them, I wish to say that your sacrifices, your dreams, and your boundless love have been my wings, lifting me higher with every word and every verse.

This book is a reflection of your lessons, your guidance, and the love that has been my constant source of inspiration. May these poems carry the essence of your hearts, just as you have carried mine.

With all my love and gratitude,

Qasim

Preface

In the journey of life, there are timeless virtues and profound lessons that guide us through both the calm and stormy times. These principles continue to hold a profound relevance regardless of the era or place. Eternal Wings is an exploration of these enduring values—lessons that have stood the test of time, that will forever empower and uplift anyone who chooses to adopt them.

Like wings that carry us across vast distances, these virtues have the power to elevate our spirits, transcend our limitations, and help us soar above the struggles of life. Whether it's the strength of never say die attitude, the power of patience, firm belief in almighty's plans, non-judgemental attitude or the freedom found in understanding, each lesson shared in these pages aims to inspire readers to embrace these qualities and rise to new heights.

In writing this book, I've sought to compile not just ideas, but a pathway—one that is timeless, compassionate, and open to all who wish to explore its depths. The world may change, but these virtues remain constant, waiting to give anyone who embraces them the wings to fly.

May these pages inspire you to discover your own wings and reach new heights in life.

Acknowledgements

I would like to express my heartfelt gratitude to those whose support, encouragement, and inspiration have played an integral role in the completion of this work.

First and foremost, I am deeply indebted to my parents and all my siblings-Nasim, Naeem, Farana and Afsana for their unconditional love, guidance, and unwavering belief in me. Their sacrifices and constant encouragement have been the foundation of my success. Without their support, none of this would have been possible.

I would also like to thank some of the greatest poets of all time and my favourites Allama Iqbal, Robert Frost and PB Shelley. I got exposed to only their limited works and it was sufficient to add values to my life. Allama Iqbal's 'Nahi Nasheman tera qasr e Sultani ke gumbad par...(you don't have to have an abode in royal palaces...), Robert Frost's 'I took the one less travelled by and that has made all the difference', PB Shelley's 'if winter Comes, can spring be far behind?'...were sufficient to evoke in me a kind of attitude that has helped me to write the poems on similar themes.

A special thanks to my School English teacher, Mr. Gaurav Jha, who played an important role in my life. His each and every word not only made me believe in myself but also filled me with so much confidence and enthusiasm. I still remember how he used to ask me to write on various topics and then rewarding me with the gifts encouraging me to even write more. His passion for literature, coupled with his dedication to fostering my love for the subject, has been instrumental in shaping my intellectual growth.

To my dearest friend, Sukoon, who is not only one of the best human beings I have met in my life but also a constant and perennial source of encouragement for me. It is no exaggeration say that even our conversations shaped my perspectives providing me with the much needed clarity in my thoughts related to many aspects of our lives.

I am fortunate to be surrounded by incredible friends who have always supported me. I thank Anjali Dagar, Indu Kumari, Kavita Meena, Priyanka Singh, Shakeeb Anwer, Abdul Majid, and Ratish Kumar for their companionship and belief in me. Each and every stanza I tried to write, they were the first to appreciate it and also came up with suggestions that were of paramount importance for me in the process of completing this book.

I am also grateful to LinhTran, my friend from Vietnam for always encouraging me to keep writing.

Not to forget Bookleaf Publishing who provided me this opportunity to give the shape of a book to my random thoughts. I thank Bookleaf from the core of my heart for all the support and encouragement.

I am truly grateful to each one of you for your unwavering support and contributions. This work stands as a testament to the invaluable influence you all have had in my life.

1. One out of Millions

Millions will come and perish but you have to stay
Against all the odds you have to make your way

The world is there to celebrate only your feats
It's only you who have to embrace your defeats

When they write you off in the very first instance
It's you who have to give yourself a second chance

And at times when all the paths seem blocked to you
Be a little patient and have unshakeable faith in you

Let perseverance and courage be your weapons
And see your pains getting eased from the heavens

And who knows a sea change may occur overnight
Miracle happen to those who persevere and who fight

Plenty of excuses to give up and only one to hold on
Hold on so that you witness altogether a new dawn

2. Judge me not

True companions come at a cost they say
I'll tell you simple rules and nothing to pay

Judge me not and accept me the way I am
And you will see what a beautiful soul I am

True that I am not perfect and full of flaws
But I keep evolving even my enemy knows

Say my insecurities are at the safest hands
And I will walk with you to the far off lands

Let me confide in you all that precious to me
Be brave enough to return all that only to me

And be my back when it all goes against me
Witness the rivers of love flowing into a sea

I bluntly say it all with nothing more to reveal
Pure souls have hardly anything to conceal

3. Thriving Together

The faces may be deceptive, the hearts are true
And you never know what one is going through

Before you judge, make sure you are gutsy enough
And that seeking forgiveness is not a job very tough

True, the fights, the battles, the struggles are his own
Put a hand on his shoulder; let him feel he is not alone

A slight push, a few soothing words and a pep up
You never know to what extent it can boost someone up

Who knows some day you might be in similar situations
And you will need those good deeds for your protection

The empathy, the encouragement, the motivation
It all may lead to outcomes beyond imagination

Let's make them an indispensable part of our lives
In such a community of dreams, everyone thrives.

4. History is all Yours

Don't pretend to be dreamless, fragile and weak
Come, look into my eyes and let your heart speak

I know your past at times came heavily on you
Smile in gratitude and feel proud for sailing through

And let those badges inspire and motivate you forever
Whenever you feel down, dejected and in despair

Time will keep testing you and stand your way
The winds with all its might will block your way

And you never learnt to succumb without a fight
Walking on a path that was just fair and upright

Let these feelings of self doubt and apprehensions
Be thrown deep into the ocean with no dimensions

That portion of the life would be cherished the most
You bounced back when everyone thought you lost

Rise, awake and go for it before it's too late
You have nothing to lose and history to create

5. Embarking on a Beautiful Journey

Eternal and everlasting not you are
Nefarious designs preparing you are
You Hold the grudges
And let the termites make you hollow
Forgive and open your arms
And that's the actual path to follow
Let silence do the talking
when the talking does not
Let inactivity win
When the dynamism does not
And embrace introspection
Instead of certifications
And allow your conscience
To perform the operations
You will surely see in that case
That you no longer carry those weights
The world becomes a beautiful place
And a beautiful journey then awaits

6. Almighty's Plans

Pondering deep over how the things unfolded
In mysterious ways the personality it moulded

Let me say it with all heart and conviction
Plans of Almighty were beyond suspicion

And at times so myopic were my views
Barely I could look to the rainbow of hues

I prayed, pleaded and aspired only for a tree
When there was a whole garden waiting for me

I complaint about hardships that came my way
And without them all my glitter would fade away

In the books of almighty nothing goes unrecorded
Don't worry all your efforts shall surely be rewarded

Starve for a soul-accountable, crystalline and pure
And that will make you a worthy creation for sure.

7. If Catharsis had a face

When someone approaches you filled with emotions Put
your hand on his shoulder; allow the ventilation

Let him cry, let him shout, let him speak his
heart out
The treatment starts from the moment he bursts it
all out

And like a perfect listener, pay heed to everything
he says
Empathise every bit of it and if required, please
paraphrase

And don't go for telling him the solutions feasible
to you
Help him to identify the roots of the problems he is
going through

Let him brainstorm and let the solutions come only from
him

Help him to gain new insights which will be the remedy
for him

8. The key to Ascension

In an imperfect world we all keep striving for perfection
Few bad decisions and we feel it's beyond resurrection

And we keep repenting when it's the time for
contemplation
Kudos for making those decisions without any hesitation

And don't be harsh to yourself, you deserve all sorts of
adoration
You made a choice when everyone thought it was
beyond imagination

And look you have already conquered your fears and
apprehensions
You have lost nothing but achieved the key to ascension

9. Be a Human Everyday

In a mad race to excel in my life
One more day passed of my life

And at the dead of this soulful night
The stars twinkling full and bright

A dry shower wrenched my face
Asking to put a halt on my pace

Plenty of questions glaring at me
And I can't dare to escape and flea

Life is unpredictable they say
Not sure if I will see another day

And therefore let me sit to reflect
Opening deeds diary to introspect

Let me recall If I was harsh and cruel
When courtesy could be the lethal tool

I seek forgiveness if I said something
Piercing someone's heart to bleeding

Did I do enough to light up the faces
Down, dejected and not ready for braces

Ultimately these are the values that I die for
Accountability of my conscience to the core

Reflecting it all, I feel I had a good day of life
I won't regret if I don't see another day of life

10. The Journey is Totally Yours

Certain journeys are only yours how difficult the terrain is
Certain battles are solely yours how powerful the enemy is

Sufferings are only for you to endure and make most of it
And expect no one to understand and empathise even an iota of it

Start now, start alone, dependency will only prolong your fight
What seems to be acute now, may become chronic a fight

Well the beginning may be a bit nasty aiming at breaking you
And once you survive, you are definitely gonna sail through

11. Destined to Rise

I don't wish to carry the burden of perfection on my
shoulders
And therefore allow me to fall, to crumble and to falter

Let me embrace those vulnerabilities glaring at me
Assuring they are companions, not enemies to me

And let me get exposed to both the cures as well as the
scars
Like a vagabond finding bliss in laying beneath the stars

And let me not be scared of the facades that come my
way
Truth, like an inevitable volcano, will ultimately make its
way

Let me not be scared of the clouds of negativity hovering
over me
Born to disperse and vanish, they can't dare to penetrate
inside me

Let me not be scared of the lows and lose my vitality
I am destined for peaks and that's the ultimate reality

12. Not Done Yet

The roads are not travelled yet
The feats are not achieved yet
Let everyone bleed, bleed and bleed
As History is not created yet

The tears are not wiped yet
The wounds are not healed yet
Let the flowers bloom, bloom and bloom
Mankind has not blossomed yet

The fragments are not united yet
Diversity is not cherished yet
Let the land progress, progress and progress
The summits are not climbed yet

The veins are not frozen yet
The wings are not broken yet
Let me promise to shine, shine and shine
I have not surrendered yet

13. Change is the only Reality

The clouds however dark, gonna disperse one day
The fog however dense, gonna disappear one day
The scars however deep, gonna heal one day
The seeds however deep, gonna sprout one day
The truth however subdued gonna prevail one day
The wait however long, gonna pay off one day
The times however tough, gonna pass one day
Have a little bit of more patience, hope and optimism
The virtues are surely going to be rewarded one day.

14. The Wings to Fly

Walking on a path so uncertain and so obscure
Plenty of sacrifices to make and a lot to endure

And a blanket of thorns waits to wrap around you
You need some great buddies as shield around you

You are bound to feel exhausted, weary and tired
Making you feel like the whole universe conspired

And therefore you need those great souls around you
To embrace you, to motivate you and to stimulate you

Putting away all your apprehensions and your fears
And wiping out all your precious drops of tears

Making you believe you are not born to be defeated
And you must not stop till the mission is completed

Let me feel blessed to have such souls around
Who, bits by bits, piece by piece, heal my wounds

They enable me to hold my head high in the sky
They are the ones who provide me the wings to fly

15. Born for Peaks

'The road is not meant for you'
'Try something you are fit to do'

'Just leave it here and move on'
' Plenty of options to look upon'

' It's not safe to play with your life'
'Putting life on the edge of a knife'

That's how the universe conspire
To extinguish inner flames of fire

But if there is a slight hope in it
Convince yourself to go for it

Let mediocrity not be your way
Let peaks be the ultimate stay

16. Wounds do Heel

You came,
You stayed,
You conquered,
You healed and
Moved away
Been quite a long
but the hangover
does not fade away
The fragrance,
the vibes,
the energy,
it all takes hold of me
And with a smile
I cherish
I rejoice
I celebrate
All that happened to me.

17. Rising from the Ashes

Deep inside the heart penetrated a faint glimmer of light
Like a hope, reviving a fragile soul with nothing in sight

Broken promises, Crushed dreams, and unmet
expectations
All coming to life and screaming out of frustrations

And with a stern look asking how I dared to quit
When the deal was to display indomitable courage and
grit

Pondered deep but went in vain the so called eloquence
And with no answer in my head, I stood in sheer
ignorance

Nothing below the pinnacle was concurred to be the
finishing line
And letting complacency to take over was no less than a
crime

The zeal, the zest, all vanished for a while if not perished
That too when a cruel history is something that I never
cherished

And it's scary to imagine a mountain losing to passing
showers
When all it could do was to help bloom the seeds to
flowers

Let the tale of ascension float and that of downfall be a
history now
Let me awake from deep slumber, to fly and fly to the
sky now

18. The Past, The Present, The Future

The past, if it was beautiful, let it remind you time and
again
That you have all the sketches to paint your life once
again

And if it was a bit excruciating, let it remind you of the
lessons
Inculcating in the life the most prized possessions

Let it be made very clear to the heart, mind and soul
That dwelling in the past is not allowed at all

Look at those lands with blooming flowers, so barren at
one point of time
Shouting that stagnancy has never been the norm of a
life so divine

The present, like a soothing breeze, is gazing from the
door

With endless opportunities, countless blessings and
much more

And let me open my arms wide enough to embrace it
with all my heart
For I know it will ultimately define the journey and will
set it apart

The future, like a chapter unread and unfamiliar and yet
so likely
Only if amidst those clouds and storms I conducted
myself uprightly

Let me decide if I wish to have, regrets, grief and sorrow
at the end of the road
Or with a smile of contentment I wish to depart for the
heavenly abode

2. I am not Afraid

I wish to smile and laugh my heart out
But I am not afraid of tears flowing out

I wish to strive hard and give it my all
But I am not afraid to plunge and fall

I wish to sail smoothly all across the sea
But I am not afraid of storms over the sea

I wish everyone to clap and cheer for me
But I am not afraid of those opposing me

I wish the spring to breathe a new life into me
But I am not afraid of the winter chasing me

I wish to embark on a journey full of prices
But I am not afraid to make those sacrifices

I wish to be on mountains that are steep
But I am not afraid of being buried deep

20. Earthly Angels

The stories of angels; quite prominent in my childhood
days
Love, affection and benevolence-their traits that I was
taught always

With wings on their back, I imagined them to fly in the
sky
Never knew the two of them stayed with me ; not in the
sky

The father, like a shield, protecting me from all the
vulnerabilities
The mother, like the ocean of love, nurturing me beyond
her abilities

The epitomes of sacrifice, resilience and compassion they
are
The universe has a dearth of vocabulary to describe what
they are

The father, known for hiding tears, cried when the child
was operated
The mother, prayed to heal him even at the cost of her
soul getting liberated

They spent their lives ensuring your well being wiping
tears from your eyes
When they grow old, please ensure not a single drop of
tear falls from their eyes

21. Crystalline Conscience

The weight of guilt, a burden so deep,
A silent cry, a soul's lost sleep.
It hangs like chains, heavy and cold,
A conscience broken, its truth untold.

For deeds and actions, the heart must bear,
A reflection of choices, the burdens we wear.
The road to goodness, not paved with ease,
No bed of roses, no gentle breeze.

It calls for a mind, a soul, a will,
To climb the mountains, to brave the chill.
With every step, through trial and fight,
The path is hard, but it leads to light.

When unrest strikes, a heart feels small,
For a life unhelped, a cry, a call.
Let intention guide, let it be true,
A compass within, for what you must do.

For conscience is shaped by the life you lead,
By the kindness sown, and the love you seed.
In every thought, in every deed,
It is the heart's intent that plants the seed.